A Book Of Poems
Of
Life And Love

T0116863

A Book Of Poems
Of
Life And Love

By Gary T. Miner

Order this book online at www.trafford.com
or email orders@trafford.com

Most Trafford titles are also available at major online book retailers.

Printed in the United States of America.

ISBN: 978-1-4269-6225-7 (sc)
ISBN: 978-1-4269-6226-4(hc)
ISBN: 978-1-4269-6227-1 (e)

Library of Congress Control Number: 2011904839

Trafford rev. 03/28/2011

 www.trafford.com

North America & international
toll-free: 1 888 232 4444 (USA & Canada)
phone: 250 383 6864 ♦ fax: 812 355 4082

Table of Contents

Dedication:

To my Mother who instilled in me the joy
of the written word, and who's love kept my
feet on the road of life when times were tough.
To my Father who's example of love, kindness
and understanding towards people has helped me
see the world and people as I do, and helped me
weather the many storms of which I write. I love
and miss them both.
To my Wife Joan Marie who walked with me hand
in hand through it all, and shared with me her love
and her life.

(Thanks Bonnie)

Hope

The shaking off of winter dreams
With thoughts and sounds of spring
Of spring and summer flower themes
And joy the warmth of day does bring

As mother nature stirs the earth
Our treasures to enjoy so sweet
Within the cycle of sleep and birth
And warm soft earth beneath our feet

On fuzzy buds our hopes do lie
And soon our hands take part
As with the sun and wind and sky
And songs of birds that take to heart

To turn our thoughts to warmth and fun
And soon we will rejoice
It takes the friendship of the sun
And songs of every garden's voice

Gary T. Miner

Journey

As I reflect upon my days
I look at life with smiles
How I've been blessed in many ways
As Joan and I have walked the miles

With everything that life does bring
Not everything is planned
It makes my heart beat loud and sing
Our strength is holding hand in hand

Together we have spent the years
In sunshine and in cloud
Through blessings and at times in tears
In love in time allowed

Friends

There are some people in this life
Our journey's made worth living
A Mother, Father, kids, a wife
With endless acts of giving

But then there is another stream
From which flows quiet love
They come to help your tears and dreams
They're sent from up above

They hide behind their everyday
When everything is well
To help when troubles' on the way
They're quick to hear the bell

These people, friends, I am truly blessed
They come without a call
When times are tough and really stressed
I truly love them all

Gary T. Miner

Mom

I struggle with my loss today
My Mom is gone she could not stay
Her love for me was life itself
There is no other greater wealth

The love God sent through her was strong
I heard her love come through her song
As I was young upon her knee
The Owl and the Pussycat went to sea

I felt that love throughout my life
And even through my times of strife
She was my Mother and she was love
That God had sent from up above

She's happy now with job well done
With Dad and family, friends and fun
I wish a message I could send
One minute more I wish to spend
So I could sit upon her knee
While the Owl and the Pussycat went to sea

Gary T. Miner

Reflections

My life is passing day by day
And there are many times I pray
To keep my family safe and warm
Please shelter them from this world's storm

I will not be forever here
To stand guard and to keep them near
Somehow I wish that they would know
That I have always loved them so

Yet in this crowd I have at home
Sometimes I feel I'm all alone
There is a sadness I endure
Because of things I am unsure

I love my Joan as no-one could
As she is kindness, love and good
I treasure every moment spent
I thank God for her love he sent

The blessings I've received are many
And never really asked for any
Except keep my family safe and warm
And shelter them from this world's storm

Gary T. Miner

Mothers Wing

There's something I would like to sing
It's safe and dry and warm
It's underneath a Mothers wing
That saves us from the storm

It's always there until the end
No safer place to be
A loving place for time to spend
It always was for me

To venture out as time goes by
Is what we all must do
We learn to trust and love and fly
And other lessons too

To sing, to laugh, to pray, be fair
That's where it came to me
My values learned when I was there
No better place to be

Gary T. Miner

Thoughts

I see her moving far away
I wish that I could make her stay
So close to me that I could see
Together Always we will be

But she is looking up ahead
To other things that I do dread
Will take her far away from me
And all alone I then will be

Without her I would not survive
And would not want to be alive
But while I'm here I wish that she
Would hover very close to me

I fear the day that I must go
I've always tried to tell her so
How wonderful our lives together
Enjoy because it's not forever

In heaven I will wait for thee
And there forever we will be
For you I know that God will send
To share our love where time won't end

Gary T. Miner

The Righteous

I learned some things about life today
To think of others is the way
When blinded by ones own desires
We flicker with damnation's fires

To preach that righteous is the goal
And all we must, to save our soul
Then act another way is wrong
How can you sing His praise's song

A mirror look we all should share
To make sure the right person's there
Because too many times we see
What's good for you is not for me

I wonder how these people face
The honest of our human race
And go among us day by day
And preach we must behave this way

Gary T. Miner

It's Time

The crosses that we all must share
Are difficult to face
It's sometimes more than we can bare
He takes us then in His embrace

So fragile is the life we live
And helpless are our minds
To understand what God did give
To much we are all blind

My heart is heavy with the thought
I cry for what I'll miss
Your eyes, your touch, the love you brought
The tenderness of your sweet kiss

The longing that we feel to stay
Is tempered by His glow
For <u>here</u>, we almost always pray
But it is time to go

Gary T. Miner

Brother

It came to me when I was sad
There's things I wish my Brother had
I wish that time could turn around
And help him find what I have found

True love, in purest, simple form
Can save us from most any storm
And happiness would mostly be
That's how it's been in life for me

I'm sending love along with this
Together with a hug and kiss
From Mom and Dad, and yes from me
For Brothers we will always be

Gary T. Miner

Life

Our time is planned our fate is set
We manage to survive and yet
There isn't much that we can do
To say but when our time is through

What faith we have must carry us
To comfort in the plan and thus
We follow through with hopes and dreams
Of this world and at times it seems

In anything that we succeed
Must be of purest thought and deed
To ponder what the timing is
The final choice of time is His

Gary T. Miner

Autumn

I'm in the autumn of my days
And I look back to see the ways
That time in Spring and Summer's past
Have gone by in a moment fast

When it was Spring I used to be
A young man with the world to see
Then Summer came and I would think
How Spring had gone in just a blink

The Summer days were warm with dreams
I cherished every day it seems
Then love came in and she would stay
A family and a house to play

Now Autumn's here and as I look
Another chapter in my book
Of dreams and joy and memories
I love the cool in Autumn's breeze

My Autumn chapter is not done
I hope there's many days of sun
So here's a message I would send
In Autumn time I'd like to spend

Gary T. Miner

I Love You

I feel the chill of winters hand
It's never timed when we had planned
So many things to say and do
In life you're really never through

So I must be content to say
I love you each and every day
So when the time for me does come
The Important message will be done

Gary T. Miner

The Road of Life

When first my feet stepped on the earth
The road was up the way
My future had begun at birth
With many paths to stray

Then guided gently down the road
With love and understanding
The seeds of which helped share the load
When life got so demanding

The path I chose had much reward
With love and family blessed
This love is why my heart has soared
I'm ready for the test

The road of life is now downhill
The test is what I live
With time left shortened further still
There's much I want to give

But if I had to choose to say
One gift from up above
I'd wish you each and everyday
The Miracle of love

Gary T. Miner

Neighborhood

When I was just a boy in jeans
I wasn't even in my teens
I thought on how my life was good
To grow up in this neighborhood

To feel secure and warm and kept
These feelings I have often wept
For others never get to touch
The life I live and love so much

Then I grew up and moved away
But quickly came right back to stay
For here was family, friends and life
What better place for kids and wife

With Mom and Dad right down the street
This neighborhood was hard to beat
Our family grew and played together
In sickness, health, all kinds of weather

The founders now are sadly gone
It's time for us to carry on
We're here where life is always good
We love life in our neighborhood

Gary T. Miner

Freedom Lost

Most of us go day by day
And never stop to ponder
How, we go and make our way
It truly is a wonder

We use these gifts without a thought
I think we take for granted
To understand the blessings brought
In prayer these seeds were planted

To move, and bend, and stretch, and turn
Not all of us can do
These freedoms I do deeply yearn
No deeper feelings' true

These gifts I've had for many years
I woke and found them gone
I've spent so many days in tears
But now I think I'm done

For this is where life's journey leads
I'll follow to the end
For He will temper all my needs
With true love He does send

Gary T. Miner

The Season

There is a special time of year
When all the world is full of cheer
A peace on earth for all to feel
It's time for all the world to heal

There is a change that makes us wonder
If God could send a bolt with thunder
To let us know that He is sad
For what we've done with what we've had

A year round wish I'd like to make
For all to give and not just take
So others could have better lives
It's good, I think we all should strive

So let's not stop and think, Let's do
And really try to follow through
For what we do for man on earth
Is why He brought His child at birth

To show us what one man can do
To lead us all to what is true
That peace on earth can yes be reached
If what we do *is* what He preached

Gary T. Miner

My Marion

I am a man of simple means
My partner in this life it seems
Lives more for me than for herself
For this I am a man of wealth

For Marion in my life has shown
I'll never have to walk alone
And right there she will always be
To guide, support and comfort me

We've walked together many miles
And shared our love and shared our smiles
With her beside me I am whole
We are just two, but share one soul

She is my love and is my friend
With love this message I would send
In love with you I will always be
For now and through eternity

Gary T. Miner

The Moons Message

I went out for a walk tonight
The clouds were thin , the moon was bright
It looked as if there had been snow
For all around was just a-glow

It made me think of older days
When moon lit nights, and sun lit days
How we were more a part of earth
Way back when man had his first birth

We've done some things as time passed by
We hurt the water, we hurt the sky
It seems as though we just don't think
And put the world right on the brink

It's time for us to make amends
Or else, for all the earth will end
We need together, not act alone
Before we lose this place called home

Gary T. Miner

A Winter Scene

It's clear and cold and bright tonight
There's frost upon new snow
The stars, on darkened sky's so bright
Seem mirrored down below

It's quiet, while the world does rest
This beauty rarely seen
No sounds do come to evening test
The snow is pure and clean

I've seen this in my winters' past
At night when all alone
It's beauty helps my waiting last
For true love to come home

Gary T. Miner

Fall Feelings

Out walking on a crisp Fall day
Some people talk to me and say
How beautiful the world we live
There's nothing that they wouldn't give

The smell of wood fires in the air
The last leaf falls, the trees are bare
Our gardens prep for winter's sleep
And all too soon the snow is deep

But for today I'll feel the breeze
And kick the leaves between the trees
I'll see white clouds in deep blue sky
And smile and think of days gone by

Gary T. Miner

To Say Good-Bye

I struggle with my day to day
The test I live is here to stay
I wish that I could turn back time
To younger days that come to mind

When youth and vigor were the thing
I look back, how I used to sing
The life and stories I did live
I think now, what I wouldn't give

The will to carry on is strong
But now it takes me much to long
To do the things that I once did
Was easy then, when just a kid

The life I had was never mine
It really was a lease of time
To show and do while I was here
The road I took not always clear

To say good-bye is very sad
But look back at the life we've had
So smile and cry and think of me
Our love together will always be

Gary T. Miner

Christmas Then..and Now

The lights shine softly on the house
How warm the colors glow
A creature stirs, it is a mouse
I listen long for.. .Ho Ho Ho

I know that I will never hear
Those famous words of lore
But peaceful are the thoughts with tear
Of Christmases before

When warm and safe were feelings then
Allowing childhood dreams
Of toys and candy coming when
It's different now it seems

My Christmas now is very clear
With peace and joy to sow
For friends and family they will hear
Now I say Ho Ho Ho

Gary T. Miner

The Path

When early in my days of youth
Not really very long in tooth
There was a path I used to know
To places I would often go

The path was topped in heavy green
Where giant berries could be seen
It took me deep upon a hill
Where earth and time were very still

I stayed a while as time went by
I caught a glimpse of deep blue sky
The peace I felt was just for me
For there was no-one near to see

I miss those days upon the hill
When earth and time stood very still
But memories of, do make me smile
I'd love to go back for a while

Gary T. Miner

Dad

He warmed the earth with gentle touch
Of which I often miss so much
He showed me how my life should be
To give to all unselfishly

I see him with his grey-haired smiles
We walked together many miles
He was Grampa and shared the joys
Of children's children and their toys

With Mom our family made a home
I never, ever felt alone
We shared his love until the end
A message I would like to send

I see the footprints left behind
They lead to love it comes to mind
It makes me think and feel the pride
We walked together side by side

Gary T. Miner

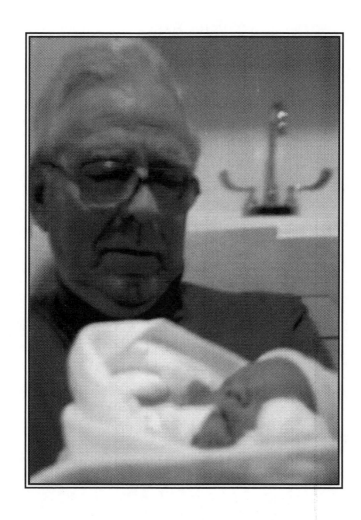

Who Am I

A wisp of Spring was in the air
I hope I'll have some time to share
Those warm and sunny days of fun
Before the days I've left are done

I've cherished early morning sky
And warm soft breeze as birds flew by
That time of day when work was done
But just before the setting sun

I've marveled at the moon at night
And thought about the sun so bright
How soft white clouds go drifting by
As floating in a deep blue sky

I hope that you can stop and see
The world as it was seen by me
And let love in as best you can
To help you understand the man

Gary T. Miner
Copyright 2010

Mom and Dad

I Often think of Mom and Dad
And I am just so very glad
That they are where they are today
Together, and that's just the way

I remember in the past
Their love I felt was meant to last
Warm memories what's left for me
I close my eyes and I can see

Their smiles, their eyes, their shinny cheek
My heart beats loud it wants to speak
But as I try it starts to break
A pause and deep breath I must take

For I must wait to see their smiles
When I have finished all my miles
For then together we will be
A Family for eternity

Gary T. Miner

I Know You

You meet some people by happenstance
But I can tell at just a glance
That beauty from within does glow
Before you have a chance to know

The air around them has a scent
That makes each moment time well spent
It makes you wish that time could freeze
Enjoy them like a summer breeze

Not many people have this touch
They're presence you enjoy so much
These folks are very rare and few
It makes me feel that I know you

Gary T. Miner

Tip

I saw a picture in different light
It's of a man, and he just might
Have seen some things I did not see
But couldn't pass them on to me

I wish now that I had the chance
To say some things that changed the dance
And shared the loves we both held dear
While we were still on earth and near

We're more alike than I once knew
Sharing dreams that fathers do
Of happiness for loved ones around
Deep in our hearts without a sound

We struggled with some days it seems
But each, we tried to fill the dreams
For those we loved and left behind
I hope some peace we all can find

Gary T. Miner

Spring Love

Oh how love used to be for me
A love so bright I could not see
The changes life does always bring
I wish I could go back to Spring

When hope and plans for life were made
Oh what I'd give if I could trade
To have that time to live again
How won-der-ful with you it's been

To snuggle warm and hold you near
Together we would never fear
The changes life does always bring
I wish I could go back to Spring

To do the things I thought were mine
But now it seems there is never time
And so the leaves begin to fall
As time comes by to touch us all
There is a wish I'd like to sing
I wish I could go back to Spring

Gary T. Miner
Copyright2010

Matthew

I see him with those soft blue eyes
The little boy inside him cries
I know the goodness in his soul
Please let him out, he's paid the toll

Although our trip has not been long
I hear in him a different song
I'ts been in him for all his life
But muffled by his times in strife

But through it all he's had the love
From Mom and Dad and up above
And some of us that he calls friend
Some comfort I would like to send

I see behind those soft blue eyes
And wish for him more sunny skies
Some peace to take along the ride
We love the Matthew deep inside

Gary T. Miner